CONVENTION
BETWEEN
THE GOVERNMENT OF THE UNITED STATES OF AMERICA
AND
THE GOVERNMENT OF THE REPUBLIC OF VENEZUELA
FOR THE AVOIDANCE OF DOUBLE TAXATION
AND THE PREVENTION OF FISCAL EVASION WITH RESPECT TO TAXES
ON INCOME AND CAPITAL

The Government of the United States of America and the Government of the Republic of

Venezuela, desiring to conclude a convention for the avoidance of double taxation and the

prevention of fiscal evasion with respect to taxes on income and capital, have agreed as follows:

ARTICLE 1

General Scope

1. This Convention shall apply to persons who are residents of one or both of the Contracting States, except as otherwise provided in the Convention.

2. The Convention shall not restrict in any manner any exclusion, exemption, deduction, credit, or other allowance now or hereafter accorded:

a) by the laws of either Contracting State; or

b) by any other agreement between the Contracting States.

3. Notwithstanding the provisions of subparagraph 2 b):

a) the provisions of Article 26 (Mutual Agreement Procedure) of this Convention exclusively shall apply to any dispute concerning whether a measure is within the scope of this Convention, and the procedures under this Convention exclusively shall apply to that dispute; and

b) unless the competent authorities determine that a taxation measure is not within the scope of this Convention, the non-discrimination obligations of this Convention exclusively shall apply with respect to that measure, except for such national treatment or most-favored-nation obligations as may apply to trade in goods under the General Agreement on Tariffs and Trade. No national treatment or most-favored-nation obligation under any other agreement shall apply with respect to that measure.

c) For the purpose of this paragraph, a "measure" is a law, regulation, rule, procedure, decision, administrative action, or any similar provision or action.

4. Notwithstanding any provision of the Convention except paragraph 5 of this Article, a Contracting State may tax its residents (as determined under Article 4 (Residence)), and by reason of citizenship may tax its citizens, as if the Convention had not come into effect.

5. The provisions of paragraph 4 shall not affect:

a) the benefits conferred by a Contracting State under paragraph 2 of Article 9 (Associated Enterprises), and under Articles 24 (Relief from Double Taxation), 25 (Non-Discrimination), and 26 (Mutual Agreement Procedure); and

b) the benefits conferred by a Contracting State under Articles 20 (Government Service), 21 (Students, Trainees, Teachers and Researchers), and 28 (Diplomatic Agents and Consular Officers), upon individuals who are neither citizens of, nor have immigrant status in, that State.

ARTICLE 2

Taxes Covered

1. The existing taxes to which this Convention shall apply are:

   a) in Venezuela: the tax on income and the business assets tax;

   b) in the United States: the Federal income taxes imposed by the Internal Revenue Code (but excluding social security contributions).

2. The Convention shall apply also to any identical or substantially similar taxes that are imposed after the date of signature of the Convention in addition to, or in place of, the existing taxes. The competent authorities of the Contracting States shall notify each other of any significant changes that have been made in their respective taxation laws and of any official published material concerning the application of the Convention.

ARTICLE 3

General Definitions

1. For the purposes of this Convention, unless the context otherwise requires:

   a) the term " Venezuela" means the Republic of Venezuela;

   b) the term "United States" means the United States of America but does not include Puerto Rico, the Virgin Islands, Guam, or any other United States possession or territory;

   c) the terms "a Contracting State" and "the other Contracting State" mean Venezuela or the United States as the context requires;

   d) the term "person" includes an individual, an estate, a trust, a partnership, a company, and any other body of persons;

e) the term "company" means any body corporate or any entity which is treated as a body corporate for tax purposes;

f) the terms "enterprise of a Contracting State" and "enterprise of the other Contracting State" mean, respectively, an enterprise carried on by a resident of a Contracting State and an enterprise carried on by a resident of the other Contracting State; the terms also include an enterprise carried on by a resident of a Contracting State through an entity that is treated as fiscally transparent in that Contracting State;

g) the term "national" means:

i) any individual possessing the nationality of a Contracting State; and

ii) any legal person, association, or other entity (including an "*entidad*" or "*colectividad*") deriving its status as such from the law in force in a Contracting State;

h) the term "international operation of ships or aircraft" means any transport by a ship or aircraft, except when such transport is solely between places within a Contracting State;

i) the term "competent authority" means:

i) in the case of the United States: the Secretary of the Treasury or his delegate; and

ii) in the case of Venezuela: the Integrated National Service of Tax Administration (Servicio Nacional Integrado de Administración Tributaria–SENIAT), its authorized representative or the authority which is designated by the Ministry of Finance as a competent authority for the purposes of this Convention.

2. As regards the application of the Convention by a Contracting State, any term not defined therein shall, unless the context otherwise requires or the competent authorities agree to a common meaning pursuant to the provisions of Article 26 (Mutual Agreement Procedure), have the meaning which it has under the laws of that State concerning the taxes to which the Convention applies.

ARTICLE 4

Residence

1. For the purposes of this Convention, the term "resident of a Contracting State" means:

    a) in the case of the United States, any person who, under the laws of the United States, is liable to tax therein by reason of his domicile, residence, citizenship, place of incorporation, or any other criterion of a similar nature. The term includes an individual who is a United States citizen or an alien lawfully admitted to the United States for permanent residence (a "green card" holder) and who is not a resident of Venezuela under paragraph 1 b) only if the individual has a permanent home or habitual abode in the United States.

    b) in the case of Venezuela, any resident individual ("*domiciliado*"), any legal person that is created or organized under the laws of Venezuela, and any entity or collectivity ("*entidad o colectividad*") formed under the laws of Venezuela which is not a legal person but is subject to the taxation applicable to corporations in Venezuela.

2. An item of income, profit or gain derived through an entity that is fiscally transparent under the laws of either Contracting State shall be considered to be derived by a resident of a State to the extent that the item is treated for purposes of the taxation law of such Contracting State as the income, profit or gain of a resident.

3. Where by reason of the provisions of paragraph 1, an individual is a resident of both Contracting States, then his status shall be determined as follows:

    a) he shall be deemed to be a resident of the State in which he has a permanent home available to him; if he has a permanent home available to him in both States, he shall be deemed to be a resident of the State with which his personal and economic relations are closer (center of vital interests);

    b) if the State in which he has his center of vital interests cannot be determined, or if he does not have a permanent home available to him in either State, he shall be deemed to be a resident of the State in which he has an habitual abode;

c) if he has an habitual abode in both States or in neither of them, he shall be deemed to be a resident of the State of which he is a national;

d) if he is a national of both States or of neither of them, the competent authorities of the Contracting States shall endeavor to settle the question by mutual agreement.

4. Where, by reason of the provisions of paragraph 1, a person other than an individual is a resident of both Contracting States, the competent authorities of the Contracting States shall endeavor to settle the question by mutual agreement and determine the mode of application of the Convention to such person. If they are unable to make such a determination, such person shall not be considered a resident of either Contracting State for purposes of enjoying benefits under this Convention.

ARTICLE 5

Permanent Establishment

1. For the purposes of this Convention, the term "permanent establishment" means a fixed place of business through which the business of an enterprise is wholly or partly carried on.

2. The term "permanent establishment" includes especially:

a) a place of management;

b) a branch;

c) an office;

d) a factory;

e) a workshop; and

f) a mine, an oil or gas well, a quarry, or any other place of extraction of natural resources.

3. The term "permanent establishment" likewise encompasses:

a) A building site or construction or installation project, or an installation or drilling rig or ship used for the exploration of natural resources, but only where such site, project or activities continue for a period or periods aggregating more than 183 days within any twelve month period commencing or ending in the taxable year concerned; and

b) The furnishing of services, including consultancy services, by an enterprise through employees or other personnel engaged by the enterprise for such purpose, but only where activities of that nature continue (for the same or a connected project) within the country for a period or periods aggregating more than 183 days in any twelve month period commencing or ending in the taxable year concerned.

4. Notwithstanding the preceding provisions of this Article, the term "permanent establishment" shall be deemed not to include:

a) the use of facilities solely for the purpose of storage, display, or delivery of goods or merchandise belonging to the enterprise;

b) the maintenance of a stock of goods or merchandise belonging to the enterprise solely for the purpose of storage, display, or delivery;

c) the maintenance of a stock of goods or merchandise belonging to the enterprise solely for the purpose of processing by another enterprise;

d) the maintenance of a fixed place of business solely for the purpose of purchasing goods or merchandise, or of collecting information, for the enterprise;

e) the maintenance of a fixed place of business solely for the purpose of carrying on, for the enterprise, any other activity of a preparatory or auxiliary character;

f) the maintenance of a fixed place of business solely for any combination of the activities mentioned in subparagraphs a) to e), provided that the overall activity of the fixed place of business resulting from this combination is of a preparatory or auxiliary character.

5. Notwithstanding the provisions of paragraphs 1 and 2, where a person–other than an agent of an independent status to whom paragraph 6 applies–is acting on behalf of an enterprise and has and habitually exercises, in a Contracting State an authority to conclude contracts in the name of the enterprise, that enterprise shall be deemed to have a permanent establishment in that State in respect of any activities which that person undertakes for the enterprise, unless the activities of such person are limited to those mentioned in paragraph 4 which, if exercised

through a fixed place of business, would not make this fixed place of business a permanent establishment under the provisions of that paragraph.

6. An enterprise shall not be deemed to have a permanent establishment in a Contracting State merely because it carries on business in that State through a broker, general commission agent, or any other agent of an independent status, provided that such persons are acting in the ordinary course of their business. However, when the activities of such an agent are devoted wholly or almost wholly on behalf of that enterprise and the transactions between the agent and the enterprise are not made under arm's length conditions, he shall not be considered an agent of independent status within the meaning of this paragraph.

7. The fact that a company which is a resident of a Contracting State controls or is controlled by a company which is a resident of the other Contracting State, or which carries on business in that other State (whether through a permanent establishment or otherwise), shall not of itself constitute either company a permanent establishment of the other.

ARTICLE 6

Income From Immovable Property (Real Property)

1. Income derived by a resident of a Contracting State from immovable property (real property), including income from agriculture or forestry, situated in the other Contracting State may be taxed in that other State.

2. The term "immovable property (real property)" shall have the meaning that it has under the law of the Contracting State in which the property in question is situated. The term shall in any case include property accessory to immovable property (real property), livestock and equipment used in agriculture and forestry, rights to which the provisions of general law respecting landed property apply, usufruct of immovable property (real property) and rights to variable or fixed payments as consideration for the working of, or the right to work, mineral deposits, sources and other natural resources. Ships, boats and aircraft shall not be regarded as immovable property (real property).

3. The provisions of paragraph 1 shall apply to income derived from the direct use, letting, or use in any other form of immovable property (real property).

4. The provisions of paragraphs 1 and 3 shall also apply to the income from immovable property (real property) of an enterprise and to income from immovable property (real property) used for the performance of independent personal services.

5. A resident of a Contracting State who is liable to tax in the other Contracting State on income from immovable property (real property) situated in the other Contracting State who is not otherwise allowed to compute the tax on such income on a net basis as if such income were business profits attributable to a permanent establishment in such other State shall be allowed to elect such treatment for any taxable year. Any such election shall be binding for the taxable year of the election and all subsequent taxable years unless the competent authority of the Contracting State in which the property is situated agrees to terminate the election.

ARTICLE 7

Business Profits

1. The business profits of an enterprise of a Contracting State shall be taxable only in that State unless the enterprise carries on business in the other Contracting State through a permanent establishment situated therein. If the enterprise carries on business as aforesaid, the business profits of the enterprise may be taxed in the other State, but only so much of them as are attributable to that permanent establishment.

2. Subject to the provisions of paragraph 4, where an enterprise of a Contracting State carries on business in the other Contracting State through a permanent establishment situated therein, there shall in each Contracting State be attributed to that permanent establishment the business profits which it might be expected to make if it were a distinct and independent enterprise engaged in the same or similar activities under the same or similar conditions.

3. Nothing in this Article shall affect the application of any law of a Contracting State relating to the determination of the tax liability of a person in cases where the information available to the competent authority of that State is inadequate to determine the profits to be attributed to a permanent establishment, provided that, on the basis of the available information, the determination of the profits of the permanent establishment is consistent with the principles stated in this Article.

4. In the determination of the business profits of a permanent establishment there shall be allowed as deductions expenses that are incurred for the purposes of the business of the permanent establishment, including executive and general administrative expenses so incurred, whether incurred in the State in which the permanent establishment is situated or elsewhere. However, no such deduction shall be allowed in respect of amounts, if any, paid (otherwise than towards reimbursement of actual expenses) by the permanent establishment to the head office of the enterprise or any of its other offices, by way of royalties, fees or other similar payments in return for the use of patents or other rights, or by way of commission for specific services performed or for management, or by way of interest on moneys lent to the permanent establishment. Likewise, no account shall be taken, in the determination of the business profits of a permanent establishment, for amounts charged (otherwise than towards reimbursement of actual expenses), by the permanent establishment to the head office of the enterprise or any of its other offices, by way of royalties, fees or other similar payments in return for the use of patents or other rights, or by way of commission for specific services performed or for management, or by way of interest on moneys lent to the head office of the enterprise or any of its other offices. A Contracting State may, consistent with its law, impose limitations on deductions, so long as these limitations are consistent with the concept of net income.

5. No business profits shall be attributed to a permanent establishment by reason of the mere purchase by that permanent establishment of goods or merchandise for the enterprise.

6. For the purposes of this Convention, the business profits to be attributed to the permanent establishment shall include only the profits or losses derived from the assets or activities of the permanent establishment and shall be determined by the same method year by year unless there is good and sufficient reason to the contrary.

7. Where business profits include items of income which are dealt with separately in other Articles of the Convention, the provisions of those Articles shall not be affected by the provisions of this Article.

8. In applying paragraphs 1 and 2 of Article 7 (Business Profits), paragraph 6 of Article 10 (Dividends), paragraph 6 of Article 11 (Interest), paragraph 4 of Article 12 (Royalties), paragraph 3 of Article 13 (Gains), Article 14 (Independent Personal Services) and paragraph 2

of Article 22 (Other Income), any income or gain attributable to a permanent establishment or fixed base during its existence is taxable in the Contracting State where such permanent establishment or fixed base is situated even if the payments are deferred until such permanent establishment or fixed base has ceased to exist.

ARTICLE 8

Shipping and Air Transport

1. Profits of an enterprise of a Contracting State from the operation of ships or aircraft in international traffic shall be taxable only in that State.

2. For the purposes of this Article, profits from the operation of ships or aircraft include profits derived from the rental of ships or aircraft on a full (time or voyage) basis. They also include profits from the rental of ships or aircraft on a bareboat basis if such ships or aircraft are operated in international traffic by the lessee, or if the rental income is incidental to profits from the operation of ships or aircraft in international traffic. Profits derived by an enterprise from the inland transport of property or passengers within either Contracting State shall be treated as profits from the operation of ships or aircraft in international traffic if such transport is undertaken as part of international traffic.

3. Profits of an enterprise of a Contracting State from the use, maintenance, or rental of containers (including trailers, barges, and related equipment for the transport of containers) used in international traffic shall be taxable only in that State.

4. The provisions of paragraphs 1 and 3 shall also apply to profits from participation in a pool, a joint business, or an international operating agency.

ARTICLE 9

Associated Enterprises

1. Where:

a) an enterprise of a Contracting State participates directly or indirectly in the management, control or capital of an enterprise of the other Contracting State; or

b) the same persons participate directly or indirectly in the management, control, or capital of an enterprise of a Contracting State and an enterprise of the other Contracting State,

and in either case, conditions are made or imposed between the two enterprises in their commercial or financial relations which differ from those that would be made between independent enterprises, then any profits that, but for those conditions, would have accrued to one of the enterprises, but by reason of those conditions have not so accrued, may be included in the profits of that enterprise and taxed accordingly.

2. Where a Contracting State includes in the profits of an enterprise of that State, and taxes accordingly, profits on which an enterprise of the other Contracting State has been charged to tax in that other State, and the profits so included are profits that would have accrued to the enterprise of the first-mentioned State if the conditions made between the two enterprises had been those that would have been made between independent enterprises, then that other State, if it agrees with such adjustment, shall make a corresponding adjustment to the amount of the tax charged therein on those profits. In determining such adjustment, due regard shall be paid to the other provisions of this Convention and the competent authorities of the Contracting States shall if necessary consult each other.

3. The provisions of paragraph 1 shall not limit any provisions of the law of either Contracting State that permit the distribution, apportionment, or allocation of income, deductions, credits, or allowances between persons, whether or not residents of a Contracting State, owned or controlled directly or indirectly by the same interests when necessary in order to prevent evasion of taxes or clearly to reflect the income of any such persons.

ARTICLE 10

Dividends

1. Dividends paid by a company that is a resident of a Contracting State to a resident of the other Contracting State may be taxed in that other State.

2. However, such dividends may also be taxed in the Contracting State of which the company paying the dividends is a resident, and according to the laws of that State, but, except

as provided in paragraph 3, if the beneficial owner of the dividends is a resident of the other Contracting State, the tax so charged shall not exceed:

a) 5 percent of the gross amount of the dividends if the beneficial owner is a company that owns at least 10 percent of the voting stock of the company paying the dividends;

b) 15 percent of the gross amount of the dividends in all other cases.

This paragraph shall not affect the taxation of the company in respect of the profits out of which the dividends are paid.

3. Subparagraph a) of paragraph 2 shall not apply in the case of dividends paid by a Regulated Investment Company (RIC) or a Real Estate Investment Trust (REIT). In the case of dividends paid by a RIC, subparagraph b) of paragraph 2 shall apply. In the case of dividends paid by a REIT, subparagraph b) of paragraph 2 also shall not apply unless:

a) the beneficial owner of the dividends is an individual holding an interest of not more than 10 percent of the REIT;

b) the dividends are paid with respect to a class of stock that is publicly traded and the beneficial owner of the dividends is a person holding an interest of not more than 5 percent of any class of the REIT's stock; or

c) the beneficial owner of the dividends is a person holding an interest of not more than 10 percent of the REIT and the REIT is diversified.

4. Notwithstanding paragraph 2, dividends may not be taxed in the Contracting State of which the company paying the dividends is a resident if the beneficial owner of the dividends is the other Contracting State or a political subdivision or local authority thereof or a resident of the other Contracting State that is a governmental entity constituted and operated exclusively to administer or provide pension benefits, provided in each case that the dividends are not derived from carrying on a trade or business or from an associated enterprise.

5. The term "dividends" as used in this Article means income from shares or other rights, not being debt-claims, participating in profits, as well as income from other corporate rights that is subjected to the same taxation treatment as income from shares by the laws of the State of which the company making the distribution is a resident. The term "dividends" also

includes income from arrangements, including debt obligations, carrying the right to participate in, or determined with reference to, profits to the extent so characterized under the laws of the Contracting State in which the income arises.

6. The provisions of paragraphs 1 and 2 shall not apply if the beneficial owner of the dividends, being a resident of a Contracting State, carries on business in the other Contracting State of which the company paying the dividends is a resident, through a permanent establishment situated therein, or performs in that other State independent personal services from a fixed base situated therein, and the dividends are attributable to such permanent establishment or fixed base. In such case the provisions of Article 7 (Business Profits) or Article 14 (Independent Personal Services), as the case may be, shall apply.

7. A Contracting State may not impose any tax on dividends paid by a company that is a resident of the other Contracting State, except insofar as the dividends are paid to a resident of that State or the dividends are attributable to a permanent establishment or a fixed base situated in that State.

ARTICLE 11

Interest

1. Interest arising in a Contracting State and derived by a resident of the other Contracting State may be taxed in that other State.

2. However, such interest may also be taxed in the Contracting State in which it arises and according to the laws of that State, but if the beneficial owner of the interest is a resident of the other Contracting State, the tax so charged shall not exceed:

a) 4.95 percent of the gross amount of the interest if the interest is beneficially owned by any financial institution (including an insurance company); and

b) 10 percent in all other cases.

3. Notwithstanding the provisions of paragraph 2, interest arising in a Contracting State shall be exempt from tax in that State if:

a) the interest is paid by that State or a political subdivision or local authority thereof;

b) the beneficial owner of the interest is the other Contracting State or a political subdivision or local authority thereof or an instrumentality wholly owned by that other State; or

c) the beneficial owner of the interest is a resident of the other State and the interest is paid with respect to debt obligations that have been made, guaranteed or insured, directly or indirectly, by that other State or a wholly owned instrumentality thereof.

4.   a) Notwithstanding the provisions of paragraph 2, interest paid by a resident of a Contracting State and that is determined with reference to receipts, sales, income, profits or other cash flow of the debtor or a related person, to any change in the value of any property of the debtor or a related person or to any dividend, partnership distribution or similar payment made by the debtor to a related person, and paid to a resident of the other State also may be taxed in the Contracting State in which it arises, and according to the laws of that State, but if the beneficial owner is a resident of the other Contracting State, the gross amount of the interest may be taxed at a rate not exceeding the rate prescribed in subparagraph b) of paragraph 2 of Article 10 (Dividends); and

b) notwithstanding the provisions of paragraphs 2 and 3, interest that is an excess inclusion with respect to a residual interest in a real estate mortgage investment conduit may be taxed by each State in accordance with its domestic law.

5. The term "interest" as used in this Convention means income from debt-claims of every kind, whether or not secured by mortgage and whether or not carrying a right to participate in the debtor's profits, and in particular, income from government securities, and income from bonds or debentures, including premiums or prizes attaching to such securities, bonds, or debentures, as well as all other income that is treated as interest by the taxation law of the Contracting State in which the income arises. Income dealt with in Article 10 (Dividends) and penalty charges for late payment shall not be regarded as interest for the purposes of the Convention.

6. The provisions of paragraphs 1, 2, 3 and 4 shall not apply if the beneficial owner of the interest, being a resident of a Contracting State, carries on business in the other Contracting

State in which the interest arises through a permanent establishment situated therein, or performs in that other State independent personal services from a fixed base situated therein, and the interest is attributable to such permanent establishment or fixed base. In such case the provisions of Article 7 (Business Profits), or Article 14 (Independent Personal Services), as the case may be, shall apply.

7. For purposes of this Article, interest shall be deemed to arise in a Contracting State when the payer is that State itself or a political subdivision, local authority, or resident of that State. Where, however, the person paying the interest, whether a resident of a Contracting State or not, has in a Contracting State a permanent establishment or a fixed base or derives profits that are taxable on a net basis in that State under paragraph 5 of Article 6 (Income From Immovable Property (Real Property)) or paragraph 1 of Article 13 (Gains), and such interest is borne by such permanent establishment or fixed base or allocable to such profits then such interest shall be deemed to arise in the State in which the permanent establishment or fixed base is situated or from which such profits are derived.

8. Where, by reason of a special relationship between the payer and the beneficial owner or between both of them and some other person, the amount of the interest, having regard to the debt-claim for which it is paid, exceeds the amount which would have been agreed upon by the payer and the beneficial owner in the absence of such relationship, the provisions of this Article shall apply only to the last-mentioned amount. In such case the excess part of the payments shall remain taxable according to the laws of each Contracting State, due regard being had to the other provisions of the Convention.

ARTICLE 11A

Branch Tax

Notwithstanding any other provisions of this Convention, a company that is a resident of a Contracting State may be subject in the other Contracting State to a tax in addition to the tax on profits. Such additional tax, however, may not exceed:

a) 5 percent of the "dividend equivalent amount" of the business profits of the company that are either attributable to a permanent establishment in that other State or are subject to tax on a net basis in that other State under Article 6 (Income From Immovable Property (Real Property)) or paragraph 1 of Article 13 (Gains); and

b) 10 percent of the "excess interest." In the case of persons referred to in subparagraph a) of paragraph 2 of Article 11 (Interest), the tax imposed under this subparagraph shall not be levied at a rate in excess of 4.95 percent.

ARTICLE 12

Royalties

1. Royalties arising in a Contracting State and derived by a resident of the other Contracting State may be taxed in that other State.

2. However, such royalties may also be taxed in the Contracting State in which they arise and according to the laws of that State, but if the beneficial owner is a resident of the other Contracting State, the tax so charged shall not exceed:

a) 5 percent of the gross amount of the royalties described in subparagraph a) of paragraph 3; and

b) 10 percent of the gross amount of the royalties described in subparagraph b) of paragraph 3.

3. The term "royalties" as used in this Convention means payments of any kind received in consideration:

a) for the use of, or the right to use, industrial, commercial, or scientific equipment; or

b) for the use of, or the right to use, any copyright of literary, dramatic, musical, artistic, or scientific work, including cinematographic films, tapes, and other means of image or sound reproduction, any patent, trademark, design or model, plan, secret formula or process, or other like right or property, or for information concerning industrial, commercial, or scientific experience. The term "royalties" also includes gains derived from the alienation of such right or property to the extent that such gains are contingent on the productivity, use, or disposition thereof.

4. The provisions of paragraphs 1 and 2 shall not apply if the beneficial owner of the royalties, being a resident of a Contracting State, carries on business in the other Contracting State, in which the royalties arise, through a permanent establishment situated therein, or performs in that other State independent personal services from a fixed base situated therein, and the royalties are attributable to such permanent establishment or fixed base. In such case the provisions of Article 7 (Business Profits) or Article 14 (Independent Personal Services), as the case may be, shall apply.

5. Royalties shall be deemed to arise in a Contracting State when they are in consideration for the use of, or the right to use, property, information or experience in that State.

6. Where, by reason of a special relationship between the payer and the beneficial owner or between both of them and some other person, the amount of the royalties, having regard to the use, right, or information for which they are paid, exceeds the amount which would have been agreed upon by the payer and the beneficial owner in the absence of such relationship, the provisions of this Article shall apply only to the last-mentioned amount. In such case the excess part of the payments shall remain taxable according to the laws of each Contracting State, due regard being had to the other provisions of the Convention.

ARTICLE 13

Gains

1. Gains or income derived by a resident of a Contracting State from the alienation of immovable property (real property) situated in the other Contracting State may be taxed in that other State.

2. For the purposes of this Article, the term "immovable property (real property) situated in the other Contracting State" includes immovable property (real property) referred to in Article 6 (Income From Immovable Property (Real Property)) that is situated in that other Contracting State and an interest in a partnership, trust or estate to the extent that its assets consist of immovable property (real property) situated in that other State. It also includes a

United States real property interest or an equivalent interest in Venezuelan immovable property (real property).

3. Gains or income from the alienation of personal (movable) property that are attributable to a permanent establishment that an enterprise of a Contracting State has in the other Contracting State, or that are attributable to a fixed base that is available to a resident of a Contracting State in the other Contracting State for the purpose of performing independent personal services, and gains or income from the alienation of such a permanent establishment (alone or with the whole enterprise) or such a fixed base, may be taxed in that other State.

4. Gains or income derived by an enterprise of a Contracting State from the alienation of ships, aircraft, or containers operated in international traffic or personal property pertaining to the operation or use of such ships, aircraft or containers shall be taxable only in that State.

5. Gains or income from the alienation of any property other than property referred to in paragraphs 1 through 4 shall be taxable only in the Contracting State of which the alienator is a resident.

ARTICLE 14

Independent Personal Services

1. Subject to the provisions of Article 7 (Business Profits), income derived by an individual who is a resident of a Contracting State in respect of professional services or similar activities of an independent character shall be taxable only in that State. However, such income may be taxed in the other Contracting State if such individual has a fixed base regularly available to him in the other Contracting State for the purpose of performing those activities. In that case, only so much of the income as is attributable to that fixed base may be taxed in that other Contracting State.

2. The term "professional services" includes especially independent scientific, literary, artistic, educational, or teaching activities as well as the independent activities of physicians, lawyers, engineers, architects, dentists, and accountants.

ARTICLE 15

Dependent Personal Services

1. Subject to the provisions of Articles 16 (Directors' Fees), 19 (Pensions, Social Security, Annuities, and Child Support), 20 (Government Service), and 21 (Students, Trainees, Teachers and Researchers), salaries, wages, and other similar remuneration derived by a resident of a Contracting State in respect of an employment shall be taxable only in that State unless the employment is exercised in the other Contracting State. If the employment is so exercised, such remuneration as is derived therefrom may be taxed in that other State.

2. Notwithstanding the provisions of paragraph 1, remuneration derived by a resident of a Contracting State in respect of an employment exercised in the other Contracting State shall be taxable only in the first-mentioned State if:

a) the recipient is present in the other State for a period or periods not exceeding in the aggregate 183 days in any twelve month period beginning or ending in the taxable year concerned;

b) the remuneration is paid by, or on behalf of, an employer who is not a resident of the other State; and

c) the remuneration is not borne by a permanent establishment or a fixed base that the employer has in the other State.

3. Notwithstanding the preceding provisions of this Article, remuneration described in paragraph 1 that is derived by a resident of a Contracting State in respect of an employment as a member of the crew of a ship or aircraft, or as other personnel regularly employed to serve aboard a ship or aircraft, operated in international traffic shall be taxable only in that State.

ARTICLE 16

Directors' Fees

Notwithstanding the provisions of Articles 14 (Independent Personal Services) and 15 (Dependent Personal Services), directors' fees and other similar payments derived by a resident of a Contracting State for services performed in the other Contracting State in his capacity as a member of the board of directors of a company which is a resident of the other Contracting State may be taxed in that other State.

ARTICLE 17

Limitation on Benefits

1. A person that is a resident of a Contracting State and derives income from the other Contracting State shall be entitled to the benefits of this Convention in that other Contracting State only if such person is:

a) an individual and would not be a resident of another country under the principles of subparagraphs a) and b) of paragraph 3 of Article 4 (Residence); or

b) a Contracting State, a political subdivision or local authority thereof, a wholly-owned instrumentality of a Contracting State, a political subdivision or local authority thereof, or a company wholly-owned, directly or indirectly, by a Contracting State, a political subdivision or local authority thereof; or

c) an entity that is a not-for-profit organization (including a pension fund or private foundation) and that, by virtue of that status, is generally exempt from income taxation in its Contracting State of residence, provided that more than half of the beneficiaries, members, or participants, if any, in such organization are entitled to the benefits of this Convention; or

d) engaged in the active conduct of a trade or business in the first-mentioned Contracting State (other than the business of making or managing investments, unless these activities are banking or insurance activities carried on by a bank or insurance company), the income derived from the other Contracting State is derived in connection with, or is incidental to, that trade or business, and the trade or business is substantial in relation to the activity carried on in the other Contracting State giving rise to the income in respect of which treaty benefits are being claimed in that other Contracting State; or

e) a company in whose principal class of shares there is substantial and regular trading on a recognized securities exchange; or

f) a company of which at least 50 percent of each class of shares in the company is owned directly or indirectly by five or fewer companies entitled to the benefits under subparagraph e), provided that in the case of indirect ownership, each intermediate owner is a person entitled to benefits of the Convention under this paragraph; or

g) both of the following conditions are satisfied:

i) more than 50 percent of the beneficial interest in such person (or in the case of a company, more than 50 percent of the number of shares of each class of the company's shares) is owned, directly or indirectly, by persons who are entitled to the benefits of the Convention under subparagraphs a), b), c), e), or f) or who are citizens of the United States; and

ii) less than 50 percent of the gross income of such person is used, directly or indirectly, to meet liabilities (including liabilities for interest or royalties) to persons who are not entitled to the benefits of the Convention under subparagraphs a), b), c), e), or f) or who are citizens of the United States.

2. Notwithstanding paragraph 1, an *entidad* or *colectividad* formed under the laws of Venezuela otherwise entitled to benefits under paragraph 1 shall not be entitled to the benefits of this Convention if that *entidad* or *colectividad*, or another *entidad* or *colectividad* or other person that controls such *entidad* or *colectividad*, has outstanding a class of interests:

a) the terms of which, or which is subject to other arrangements that, entitle its holders to a portion of the income of the *entidad* or *colectividad* derived from the United States that is larger than the portion such holders would receive absent such terms or arrangements; and

b) 50 percent or more of the vote or value of which is owned by persons who are not persons entitled to the benefits of this Convention under subparagraphs a), b), c), e), or f) of paragraph 1 or citizens of the United States.

3. Notwithstanding paragraph 1, a former long-term resident of the United States shall not be entitled to the benefits of this Convention for the 10-year period following loss of such status, if such loss had for one of its principal purposes the avoidance of U.S. tax, determined in

accordance with the provisions of United States law applicable to former U.S. citizens and long-term residents.

4. A person that is not entitled to the benefits of the Convention pursuant to the provisions of paragraph 1 may, nevertheless, demonstrate to the competent authority of the State in which the income arises that such person should be granted the benefits of the Convention. For this purpose, one of the factors the competent authorities shall take into account is whether the establishment, acquisition, and maintenance of such person and the conduct of its operations did not have as one of its principal purposes the obtaining of benefits under the Convention.

5. For purposes of subparagraph e) of paragraph 1, the term "recognized securities exchange" means:

a) the Caracas and Maracaibo stock exchanges, the Bolsa Electrónica and any stock exchange registered with the Comisión Nacional de Valores in accordance with the Ley de Mercado de Capitales;

b) the NASDAQ System owned by the National Association of Securities Dealers, Inc. and any stock exchange registered with the Securities and Exchange Commission as a national securities exchange for purposes of the Securities Exchange Act of 1934; and

c) any other stock exchange agreed upon by the competent authorities of the Contracting States.

6. For purposes of subparagraph g) ii) of paragraph 1, the term "gross income" means gross receipts, or where an enterprise is engaged in a business which includes the manufacture or production of goods, gross receipts reduced by the direct costs of labor and materials attributable to such manufacture or production and paid or payable out of such receipts.

ARTICLE 18

Artistes and Sportsmen

1. Income derived by a resident of a Contracting State as an entertainer, such as a theater, motion picture, radio, or television artiste, or a musician, or as a sportsman, from his

personal activities as such exercised in the other Contracting State, which income may be exempt from tax in that other Contracting State under the provisions of Articles 14 (Independent Personal Services) and 15 (Dependent Personal Services), may be taxed in that other State except where the amount of the compensation derived by such entertainer or sportsman, including expenses reimbursed to him or borne on his behalf, from such activities does not exceed six thousand United States dollars ($6,000) or its equivalent in Venezuelan bolívares for the taxable year concerned.

2. Where income in respect of activities exercised by an entertainer or a sportsman in his capacity as such accrues not to the entertainer or sportsman but to another person, that income of that other person may, notwithstanding the provisions of Articles 7 (Business Profits) and 14 (Independent Personal Services), be taxed in the Contracting State in which the activities of the entertainer or sportsman are exercised, unless it is established that neither the entertainer or sportsman nor persons related thereto participate directly or indirectly in the profits of that other person in any manner, including the receipt of deferred remuneration, bonuses, fees, dividends, partnership distributions, or other distributions.

3. The provisions of paragraphs 1 and 2 shall not apply to income derived from activities performed in a Contracting State as an entertainer or sportsman if the visit to that State is wholly or mainly supported by public funds of one or both of the Contracting States or political subdivisions or local authorities thereof. In such a case, the income is taxable only in the Contracting State of which the artiste or sportsman is a resident.

ARTICLE 19

Pensions, Social Security, Annuities, and Child Support

1. Subject to the provisions of Article 20 (Government Service), pensions and other similar remuneration derived and beneficially owned by a resident of a Contracting State in consideration of past employment shall be taxable only in that State.

2. Social security benefits paid by a Contracting State to a resident of the other Contracting State or a citizen of the United States may be taxed in the first-mentioned State.

3. Annuities, other than those covered in paragraph 1, that are derived from a Contracting State and beneficially owned by an individual resident of the other Contracting State shall be taxable only in the first-mentioned State. The term "annuities" as used in this paragraph means a stated sum paid periodically at stated times during a specific time period, under an obligation to make the payments in return for adequate and full consideration (other than services rendered).

4. Periodic payments for the support of a minor child made pursuant to a written separation agreement or a decree of divorce, separate maintenance, or compulsory support, paid by a resident of a Contracting State to a resident of the other Contracting State, shall be taxable only in that other State.

ARTICLE 20

Government Service

1.　　a) Remuneration, other than a pension, paid by a Contracting State or a political subdivision or a local authority thereof to an individual in respect of services rendered to that State or subdivision or authority shall be taxable only in that State.

b) However, such remuneration shall be taxable only in the other Contracting State if the services are rendered in that State and the individual is a resident of that State who:

i) is a national of that State; or

ii) did not become a resident of that State solely for the purpose of rendering the services.

2. Subject to the provisions of paragraph 2 of Article 19 (Pensions, Social Security, Annuities, and Child Support):

a) Any pension paid by, or out of funds created by, a Contracting State or a political subdivision or a local authority thereof to an individual in respect of services rendered to that State or subdivision or authority shall be taxable only in that State.

b) However, such pension shall be taxable only in the other Contracting State if the individual is a resident of, and a national of, that State.

3. The provisions of Articles 14 (Independent Personal Services), 15 (Dependent Personal Services), 16 (Directors' Fees), 18 (Artistes and Sportsmen), and 19 (Pensions, Social Security, Annuities, and Child Support) shall apply to remuneration and pensions in respect of services rendered in connection with a business carried on by a Contracting State or a political subdivision or a local authority thereof.

ARTICLE 21

Students, Trainees, Teachers and Researchers

1.   a) Except as provided in paragraph 2, an individual who is a resident of a Contracting State at the beginning of his visit to the other Contracting State and who is temporarily present in that other Contracting State for the primary purpose of :

i) studying at a university or other recognized educational institution in that other Contracting State, or

ii) securing training required to qualify him to practice a profession or professional specialty, or

iii) studying or doing research as a recipient of a grant, allowance, or award from a governmental, religious, charitable, scientific, literary, or educational organization,

shall be exempt from tax by that other Contracting State with respect to the amounts described in subparagraph b) of this paragraph for a period not exceeding 5 taxable years from the date of his arrival in the other Contracting State, and for such additional period of time as is necessary to complete, as a full-time student, educational requirements as a candidate for a postgraduate or professional degree from a recognized educational institution.

b) The amounts referred to in subparagraph a) of this paragraph are:

i) payments from abroad, other than compensation for personal services, for the purpose of his maintenance, education, study, research, or training;

ii) the grant, allowance, or award; and

iii) income from personal services performed in that other Contracting State in an aggregate amount not in excess of five thousand United States dollars ($5,000) or its equivalent in Venezuelan bolívares for the taxable year concerned.

2. An individual who is a resident of a Contracting State at the beginning of his visit to the other Contracting State and who is temporarily present in that other Contracting State as an employee of, or under contract with, a resident of the first-mentioned Contracting State, for the primary purpose of:

a) acquiring technical, professional, or business experience from a person other than that resident of the first-mentioned Contracting State, or

b) studying at a university or other recognized educational institution in that other Contracting State,

shall be exempt from tax by that other Contracting State for a period not to exceed 12 months with respect to his income from personal services in an aggregate amount not in excess of eight thousand United States dollars ($8,000) or its equivalent in Venezuelan bolívares.

3. An individual who is a resident of a Contracting State at the beginning of his visit to the other Contracting State and who is temporarily present in the other Contracting State for the purpose of teaching or carrying on research at a recognized educational or research institution shall be exempt from tax in the other Contracting State on his income from personal services for teaching or research at such institution for a period not exceeding two years from the date of the individual's arrival in that other State. In no event shall any individual have the benefits of this paragraph for more than five taxable years.

4. This Article shall not apply to income from research if such research is undertaken not in the public interest but primarily for the private benefit of a specific person or persons.

ARTICLE 22

Other Income

1. Items of income of a resident of a Contracting State, wherever arising, not dealt with in the foregoing Articles of this Convention shall be taxable only in that State.

2. The provisions of paragraph 1 shall not apply to income, other than income from immovable property (real property) as defined in paragraph 2 of Article 6 (Income From Immovable Property (Real Property)), if the recipient of such income, being a resident of a Contracting State, carries on business in the other Contracting State through a permanent establishment situated therein, or performs in that other State independent personal services from a fixed place situated therein, and the right or property in respect of which the income is paid is attributable to such permanent establishment or fixed base. In such case the provisions of Article 7 (Business Profits) or Article 14 (Independent Personal Services), as the case may be, shall apply.

3. Notwithstanding the provisions of paragraphs 1 and 2, items of income of a resident of a Contracting State not dealt with in the foregoing Articles of this Convention and arising in the other Contracting State may also be taxed in that other State.

ARTICLE 23

Capital

1. Capital represented by immovable property (real property) referred to in Article 6 (Income From Immovable Property (Real Property)), owned by a resident of a Contracting State and situated in the other Contracting State, may be taxed in that other State.

2. Capital represented by personal (movable) property forming part of the business property of a permanent establishment that an enterprise of a Contracting State has in the other Contracting State, or by personal (movable) property pertaining to a fixed base available to a resident of a Contracting State in the other Contracting State for the purpose of performing independent personal services, may be taxed in that other State.

3. Capital represented by ships, aircraft, and containers owned by a resident of a Contracting State and used in international operations, and by personal (movable) property pertaining to the operation of such ships, aircraft, and containers shall be taxable only in that State.

4. All other elements of capital of a resident of a Contracting State shall be taxable only in that State.

ARTICLE 24

Relief from Double Taxation

1. It is understood that double taxation will be avoided in accordance with the following paragraphs of this Article.

2. When a resident of Venezuela derives income that, in accordance with the provisions of this Convention, may be taxed in the United States, Venezuela shall allow a relief to such resident. Such relief shall be allowed in accordance with the provisions and subject to the limitations of the law of Venezuela, as they may be amended from time to time without changing the principle hereof. The relief may consist alternatively of:

      a) an exemption of such income from Venezuelan tax, or

      b) a credit against the Venezuelan tax on income.

3. The United States shall allow to a resident or citizen of the United States as a credit against the United States tax on income:

      a) the income tax paid to Venezuela by or on behalf of such citizen or resident; and

      b) in the case of a United States company owning at least 10 percent of the voting stock of a company which is a resident of Venezuela and from which the United States company receives dividends, the income tax paid to Venezuela by or on behalf of the distributing company with respect to the profits out of which the dividends are paid.

Such credit shall be allowed in accordance with the provisions and subject to the limitations of the law of the United States (as it may be amended from time to time without changing the general principle hereof).

ARTICLE 25

Non-Discrimination

1. Nationals of a Contracting State shall not be subjected in the other Contracting State to any taxation or any requirement connected therewith which is other or more burdensome than the taxation and connected requirements to which nationals of that other State in the same circumstances are or may be subjected. This provision shall, notwithstanding the provisions of

Article 1 (General Scope), also apply to persons who are not residents of one or both of the Contracting States.

2. The taxation on a permanent establishment which an enterprise of a Contracting State has in the other Contracting State shall not be less favorably levied in that other State than the taxation levied on enterprises of that other State carrying on the same activities. This provision shall not be construed as obliging a Contracting State to grant to residents of the other Contracting State any personal allowances, reliefs, and reductions for taxation purposes on account of civil status or family responsibilities which it grants to its own residents.

3. Nothing in this Article shall be construed as preventing either Contracting State from imposing a tax as described in Article 11A (Branch Tax).

4. Except where the provisions of paragraph 1 of Article 9 (Associated Enterprises), paragraph 8 of Article 11 (Interest), or paragraph 6 of Article 12 (Royalties) apply, interest, royalties, and other disbursements paid by an enterprise of a Contracting State to a resident of the other Contracting State shall, for the purposes of determining the taxable profits of such enterprise, be deductible under the same conditions as if they had been paid to a resident of the first-mentioned State. Similarly, any debts of a resident of a Contracting State to a resident of the other Contracting State shall, for the purpose of determining the taxable capital of the first-mentioned resident, be deductible under the same conditions as if they had been contracted to a resident of the first-mentioned State.

5. Enterprises of a Contracting State, the capital of which is wholly or partly owned or controlled, directly or indirectly, by one or more residents of the other Contracting State, shall not be subjected in the first-mentioned State to any taxation or any requirement connected therewith which is other or more burdensome than the taxation and connected requirements to which other similarly situated enterprises of the first-mentioned State are or may be subjected.

6. The provisions of this Article shall, notwithstanding the provisions of Article 2 (Taxes Covered), apply to taxes of every kind and description imposed by a Contracting State or a political subdivision or local authority thereof.

ARTICLE 26

Mutual Agreement Procedure

1. Where a person considers that the actions of one or both of the Contracting States result or will result for him in taxation not in accordance with the provisions of this Convention, he may, irrespective of the remedies provided by the domestic law of those States, and the time limits prescribed in such laws for presenting claims for refund, present his case to the competent authority of either Contracting State.

2. The competent authority shall endeavor, if the objection appears to it to be justified and if it is not itself able to arrive at a satisfactory solution, to resolve the case by mutual agreement with the competent authority of the other Contracting State, with a view to the avoidance of taxation which is not in accordance with the Convention. Provided that the statute of limitations has been interrupted in accordance with the steps designated by domestic law, any agreement reached shall be implemented and complied with, notwithstanding any time limits or other procedural limitations in the domestic laws of the Contracting States.

3. The competent authorities of the Contracting States shall endeavor to resolve by mutual agreement any difficulties or doubts arising as to the interpretation or application of the Convention. In particular, the competent authorities of the Contracting States may agree:

a) to the same allocation of income, deductions, credits, or allowances of an enterprise of a Contracting State to its permanent establishment situated in the other Contracting State;

b) to the same allocation of income, deductions, credits, or allowances between persons;

c) to the same characterization of particular items of income;

d) to the same application of source rules with respect to particular items of income;

e) to a common meaning of a term;

f) to increases in any specific amounts referred to in the Convention to reflect economic or monetary developments; and

g) to the application of the provisions of domestic law regarding penalties, fines, and interest in a manner consistent with the purposes of the Convention.

They may also consult together for the elimination of double taxation in cases not provided for in the Convention.

4. The competent authorities of the Contracting States may communicate with each other directly for the purpose of reaching an agreement in the sense of the preceding paragraphs.

ARTICLE 27

Exchange of Information

1. The competent authorities of the Contracting States shall exchange such information as is necessary for carrying out the provisions of this Convention or of the domestic laws of the Contracting States concerning taxes covered by the Convention insofar as the taxation thereunder is not contrary to the Convention. The exchange of information is not restricted by Article 1 (General Scope). Any information received by a Contracting State shall be treated as secret in the same manner as information obtained under the domestic laws of that State and shall be disclosed only to persons or authorities (including courts and administrative bodies) involved in the assessment, collection, or administration of, the enforcement or prosecution in respect of, or the determination of appeals in relation to, the taxes covered by the Convention or the oversight of the above. Such persons or authorities shall use the information only for such purposes. They may disclose the information in public court proceedings or in judicial decisions.

2. In no case shall the provisions of paragraph 1 be construed so as to impose on a Contracting State the obligation:

a) to carry out administrative measures at variance with the laws and administrative practice of that or of the other Contracting State;

b) to supply information that is not obtainable under the laws or in the normal course of the administration of that or of the other Contracting State;

c) to supply information that would disclose any trade, business, industrial, commercial, or professional secret or trade process, or information the disclosure of which would be contrary to public policy.

3. If information is requested by a Contracting State in accordance with this Article, the other Contracting State shall obtain the information to which the request relates in the same manner and to the same extent as if the tax of the first-mentioned State were the tax of that other State and were being imposed by that other State. If specifically requested by the competent authority of a Contracting State, the competent authority of the other Contracting State shall provide information under this Article in the form of depositions of witnesses and authenticated copies of unedited original documents (including books, papers, statements, records, accounts, and writings), to the same extent such depositions and documents can be obtained under the laws and administrative practices of that other State with respect to its own taxes.

4. For the purposes of this Article, the Convention shall apply, notwithstanding the provisions of Article 2 (Taxes Covered), to taxes of every kind imposed by a Contracting State.

ARTICLE 28

Diplomatic Agents and Consular Officers

Nothing in this Convention shall affect the fiscal privileges of diplomatic agents or consular officers under the general rules of international law or under the provisions of special agreements.

ARTICLE 29

Entry Into Force

1. This Convention shall be subject to ratification in accordance with the applicable procedures of each Contracting State. Each Contracting State shall notify the other through the diplomatic channel, accompanied by an instrument of ratification, when it has completed the required procedures.

2. The Convention shall enter into force upon the date of the later of the notifications, accompanied by an instrument of ratification, referred to in paragraph 1, and its provisions shall have effect:

a) in respect of taxes withheld at source, for amounts paid or credited on or after January 1 of the year following the date on which the Convention enters into force;

b) in respect of other taxes, for taxable periods beginning on or after January 1 of the year following the date on which the Convention enters into force.

ARTICLE 30

Termination

1. This Convention shall remain in force until terminated by a Contracting State. Either Contracting State may terminate the Convention at any time after five years from the date on which the Convention enters into force, provided that at least six months prior notice of the termination has been given through the diplomatic channel. In such event, the Convention shall cease to have effect:

a) in respect of taxes imposed in accordance with Articles 10 (Dividends), 11 (Interest), and 12 (Royalties), for amounts paid or credited on or after January 1 of the year following the date on which the notice is given; and

b) in respect of other taxes, for taxable periods beginning on or after January 1 of the year following the date on which the notice is given.

2. The appropriate authority of either Contracting State may request consultations with the appropriate authority of the other Contracting State to determine whether amendment to the Convention is appropriate to respond to changes in the law or policy of either Contracting State. If these consultations determine that the effect of the Convention or its application have been unilaterally changed by reason of domestic legislation enacted by a Contracting State such that the balance of benefits provided by the Convention has been significantly altered, the authorities shall consult with each other with a view to amending the Convention to restore an appropriate balance of benefits.

IN WITNESS WHEREOF, the undersigned, being duly authorized by their respective Governments, have signed this Convention.

DONE at Caracas, in duplicate, in the English and Spanish languages, each text being equally authentic, this _____ day of _____, 199_.

FOR THE GOVERNMENT OF THE   FOR THE GOVERNMENT OF
UNITED STATES OF AMERICA: THE REPUBLIC OF VENEZUELA:

PROTOCOL

At the signing today of the Convention between the Government of the United States of America and the Government of the Republic of Venezuela for the Avoidance of Double Taxation and the Prevention of Fiscal Evasion with Respect to Taxes on Income and Capital, the Contracting States have agreed upon the following provisions, which shall form an integral part of the Convention.

1.   With reference to paragraph 4 of Article 1 (General Scope)

For purposes of U.S. tax, the term "citizen" shall include a former U.S. citizen whose loss of such status had as one of its principal purposes the avoidance of U.S. tax, but only for a period of 10 years following such loss.

2.   With reference to paragraph 1a) and b) of Article 3 (General Definitions)

For the sole purposes of this Convention, when referred to in a geographical sense, Venezuela and the United States include the areas of the seabed and subsoil adjacent to their respective territorial seas in which they may exercise rights in accordance with domestic legislation and with international law.

3.   With reference to paragraph 1 of Article 4 (Residence)

The term "resident of a Contracting State" shall also include:

a) a Contracting State or a political subdivision or local authority thereof; and

b) a pension trust or any other organization that is constituted and operated exclusively to provide pension benefits or for religious, charitable, scientific, artistic, cultural, or educational purposes and that is a resident of that State according to its laws, notwithstanding that all or part of its income may be exempt from income tax under the domestic law of that State.

4.   With reference to subparagraph a) of paragraph 3 of Article 5 (Permanent Establishment)

a) It is understood that, if an enterprise (general contractor) that has undertaken the performance of a comprehensive project subcontracts parts of such project to a subcontractor, time spent by such subcontractor must be considered as time spent by the general contractor. The subcontractor has a permanent establishment only if its activities last more than 183 days in any twelve month period commencing or ending in the taxable year concerned.

b) The 183 day period begins as of the date on which the construction activity itself begins; it does not take into account time spent solely on preparatory activities, such as obtaining permits.

5.   With reference to paragraph 4 of Article 5 (Permanent Establishment)

It is understood that, in order for paragraph 4 of Article 5 (Permanent Establishment) to apply, the activities listed in subparagraphs 4 a) through f) and conducted by the resident of a Contracting State must each be of a preparatory or auxiliary character. Therefore, maintaining sales personnel in a Contracting State would not be an activity excepted under paragraph 4 and, subject to paragraphs 1, 5 and 6 of Article 5 (Permanent Establishment), would constitute a permanent establishment.

6.   With reference to paragraph 4 of Article 7 (Business Profits)

Expenses allowed as a deduction include a reasonable allocation of expenses, including executive and general administrative expenses, research and development expenses, interest, and other expenses, incurred in the taxable year for the purposes of the enterprise as a whole (or the part thereof which includes the permanent establishment), regardless of where incurred, but only to the extent that such expenses have not been deducted by such enterprise and are not reflected in other deductions allowed to the permanent establishment, such as the deduction for the cost of goods sold or of the value of the purchases. The allocation of such expenses must be accomplished in a manner that reflects to a reasonably close extent the factual relationship between the deduction and the permanent establishment and the enterprise. In determining the allocation of a specific deduction to the permanent establishment, examples of bases and factors which may be considered include, but are not limited to:

a) comparison of units sold,

b) comparison of the amount of gross sales or receipts,

c) comparison of costs of goods sold,

d) comparison of profit contribution,

     e) comparison of expenses incurred, assets used, salaries paid, space utilized, and time spent which are attributable to the activities of the permanent establishment, and

     f) comparison of the amount of gross income.

Research and development expense incurred with respect to the same product line may be allocated to a permanent establishment based on a ratio of the gross receipts of the permanent establishment to the total gross receipts of the enterprise with respect to that product line. Venezuela will not provide a deduction with respect to any expenses allocable to income not subject to tax in Venezuela because of its territorial system of taxation.

7.   With reference to Article 8 (Shipping and Air Transport)

The provisions of Article 8 (Shipping and Air Transport) shall not affect the provisions of the Agreement of December 29, 1987, between the Government of the United States of America and the Government of the Republic of Venezuela for the avoidance of double taxation with respect to shipping and air transport.

8.   With reference to Article 10 (Dividends)

It is understood that the reference in Article 10 (Dividends) paragraph 4 to "a governmental entity constituted and operated exclusively to administer or provide pension benefits" shall include, in the case of Venezuela, private, public or mixed entities operating under or pursuant to the Ley del Subsistema de Pensiones, enacted under the Ley Orgánica del Sistema de Seguridad Social Integral, so long as the system under which the entities are operating provides universal coverage; requires mandatory contributions by both employers and employees; limits the discretion of employers or employees to direct investment; restricts distributions or borrowings, directly or indirectly, except upon or until death, retirement or disability; and requires that accounts be maintained at only one such qualifying entity at a time. Such entities also must be operated, and their investment parameters established, pursuant to governmental oversight and regulation. The term also shall include any equivalent entities in the United States.

9.   With reference to Article 11 (Interest)

The instrumentalities referred to in paragraph 3 shall include the U.S. Export-Import Bank, the Federal Reserve Banks and the Overseas Private Investment Corporation, the Venezuelan Banco de Comercio Exterior, the Banco Central de Venezuela and the Fondo de Inversiones de Venezuela and such other instrumentalities as the competent authorities may agree upon.

10.   With reference to Article 11A (Branch Tax)

a) In the case of the United States the term "dividend equivalent amount" shall have the meaning it has under the laws of the United States, as it may be amended from time to time without changing the general principle thereof.

b) The term "excess interest" means the excess, if any, of:

i) interest deductible in one or more taxable years in computing the corporation's profits that are either attributable to a permanent establishment in the other Contracting State or subject to tax in that other State under Article 6 (Income From Immovable Property (Real Property)) or Article 13 (Gains), over

ii) the interest paid by or from such permanent establishment or trade or business.

11.   With reference to paragraph 3 of Article 12 (Royalties)

Payments received as consideration for technical services or assistance, including studies or surveys of a scientific, geological or technical nature, for engineering works including the plans related thereto, or for consultancy or supervisory services or assistance shall be considered payments to which the provisions of Article 7 (Business Profits) or Article 14 (Independent Personal Services) apply.

12.   With reference to Article 14 (Independent Personal Services)

Article 14 (Independent Personal Services) shall be interpreted according to the Commentary on Article 14 (Independent Personal Services) of the 1992 Model Convention for the Avoidance of Double Taxation with Respect to Taxes on Income and on Capital of the Organization for Economic Cooperation and Development, and of any guidelines which, for the application of such Article, may be developed in the future. Accordingly, it is understood that the tax will be imposed on net income as if the income were attributable to a permanent establishment and taxable under Article 7 (Business Profits).

13. With reference to Article 15 (Dependent Personal Services) and Article 16 (Directors' Fees)

The terms "similar remuneration" and "similar payments" include benefits in kind received in respect of an employment and any other benefits, whether or not considered as salary in the domestic legislation of both Contracting States (including, but not limited to, the use of a residence or automobile, health or life insurance coverage and club memberships, provision of meals, food and groceries, child care, reimbursement of medical, pharmaceutical and dental care expenses, provision of work clothing, toys and school supplies, scholarships, reimbursement of training course expenses, mortuary and burial expenses).

14. With reference to paragraph 3 of Article 17 (Limitation on Benefits)

The term "long-term resident" shall mean any individual who is a lawful permanent resident of the United States in 8 or more taxable years during the preceding 15 taxable years. In determining whether the threshold in the preceding sentence is met, there shall not count any year in which the individual is treated as a resident of Venezuela under this Convention, or as a resident of any country other than the United States under the provisions of any other tax treaty of the United States, and, in either case, the individual does not waive the benefits of such treaty applicable to residents of the other country.

15. With reference to paragraph 2 of Article 19 (Pensions, Social Security, Annuities, and Child Support)

The term "social security benefits" as used in this paragraph is intended to include United States tier 1 Railroad Retirement benefits.

16. With reference to Article 21 (Students, Trainees, Teachers and Researchers)

The amounts specified in paragraphs 1 b) iii) and 2 shall be in addition to any personal exemption otherwise allowed under the domestic law of that other Contracting State.

17.   With respect to paragraph 1 of Article 25 (Non-Discrimination)

It is understood that a non-resident of a Contracting State who is subject to tax by that State on his worldwide income by reason of being a national thereof is not in the same circumstances as a non-resident of that State who is subject to tax on income only from sources in that State.

18.   With respect to paragraph 2 of Article 26 (Mutual Agreement Procedure)

The competent authorities shall endeavor to resolve such cases as promptly as possible.

19.   With respect to Article 27 (Exchange of Information)

It is understood that in order to comply with the provisions contained in Article 27 (Exchange of Information) the competent authorities of the Contracting States are empowered by their respective domestic laws to obtain information held by persons other than taxpayers, including information held by financial institutions, agents and trustees.

IN WITNESS WHEREOF, the undersigned, being duly authorized by their respective Governments, have signed this Protocol.

DONE at Caracas, in duplicate, in the English and Spanish languages, each text being equally authentic, this _____ day of _____, 199_.

FOR THE GOVERNMENT OF THE
UNITED STATES OF AMERICA:

FOR THE GOVERNMENT OF
THE REPUBLIC OF VENEZUELA: